The Geoe

Adaptation of the spinning feelings technique

Developed by

Jihad Abou Zeid

NLP Master Practitioner & Trainer

Creator of the New Generation of NLP

Shape your feelings

Jihad Abou Zeid   www.FikrTraining.com

Intro

NLP (Neuro Linguistic Programming) has been used as a therapy to help countless people overcome fears, phobias, limiting beliefs, and many other issues. NLP has been instrumental in creating immediate change in many people's lives.

During my practice, I have found that many people had a lot of issues related to childhood or to past events. These issues usually manifest themselves as negative feelings and in many circumstances as physical pains.

While using classical NLP techniques can help in many cases, I found out that extreme cases needed more than the usual classical NLP technique.

Therefore there was a need for new more effective techniques that can help people in extreme difficult situations to feel immediate relief and to overcome the challenges, memories and painful feelings, and to replace them with calmness, relief and relaxation.

To disassociate with such memories or past events, doesn't always remove the resulting associated physical pains or emotional stress and even depression.

In these few pages, I will detail a new technique that was developed by myself as a therapy for extreme cases of stress, and emotional tension, and even depression.

Spinning Feelings

Taking the Spinning Feelings method from Nick Kemp, which is an adaptation of Richard Bandler's Spinning feelings technique, and adapting it still further has helped 100% of my clients to get immediate relief within one session.

While Richard Bandler describes the feelings as spinning and moving in a loop, few of my clients described that the feeling moved in a circle or moved back in a loop.

Richard Bandler then asks the client to take the feeling outside their body, flip it over to change its spinning direction and then put it back into their body.

 Nick Kemp, does not follow Bandler's loop movement, nor does he ask the client to remove the

Jihad Abou Zeid   www.FikrTraining.com

feeling out of their body and flip it over. Instead he lets them trace the movement of the feeling from start to end, and then asks the client to notice the direction of the spin and to take note of any color. He then asks the client to reverse the direction of the spin and to change the color to a favorite color and add some sparks.

This results in immediate relief for the clients. The addition of a favorite color involves the subconscious mind in the process of change, and the sparkles give a good feeling to clients.

Geometric Shapes

What I did was take the technique a little bit further. I start by asking the client to illicit the state where the feeling of stress or anxiety is triggered. I then ask them to describe the feeling.

Jihad Abou Zeid   www.FikrTraining.com

I draw out a sketch of the person's body, and then ask the client to draw out the path of the feeling. Where it starts, how and where it moves and where it ends its path.

As they draw and describe the feelings, I ask them to describe the shape and the color of the feeling. If the client responds with 'I don't know', I then ask them to close their eyes and take a closer look.

Once they describe a shape, movement, path and color, I simply ask them to close their eyes, then to take the shape of the feeling and change it into a different geometric shape.

For example, if they describe the feeling as triangular, I ask them to make it into circles, and let the feeling to slowly change into circular bubbles and then float off and pop out like soda bubbles and disappear. At the same time I ask them to give it a favorite color, same as in Nick Kemp's method.

Usually this works like wonders, and the client immediately feels relieved and comfortable. Quite often the client will burst out into laughter when I mention bubbles and soda.

Waves of the Ocean

I don't always use the bubbles, instead I might ask the client to change the feelings shape into waves, and give it the sound of the ocean and add a color of their choice. As the feeling starts to move in the shape of waves, I ask them to slow down the movement, and relax the waves until they are smooth and just disappear as would the waves onto the sandy beaches.

Again this technique works instantly. The negative feelings of anxiety, stress or depression disappear immediately, and get replaced with calm and relaxing feelings. Anxiety disappears and all other symptoms like heavy breathing, sweating, intensity, physical pains also disappear and are replaced by relaxed feelings.

Success Rate

Follow up with clients has always shown that the change is permanent, and the technique has 100% success rate even in very difficult situations.

In several clients, the anxiety and stress was causing physical pains in various different places in the body, mostly in the neck, shoulders and back.

The technique seems to cure these pains, which suddenly disappeared, and the clients reported complete relief from these pains without any medication. Also clients reported sleeping better at night, and many have reported that insomnia has become a thing of the past.

While many NLP therapists use the spinning feelings technique with Hypnosis, I personally never use hypnosis with NLP. I am a fan of pure NLP to affect immediate change in people's lives.

Many other NLP therapists have used the spinning feelings technique on its own and have enjoyed great results.

On the other hand, I prefer to use the technique as part of an overall therapy using a combination of techniques depending on the individual case I am dealing with, and on the severity of the case.

I also prefer to call it 'The Geometric Technique' in reference to changing the shape of the feeling, rather than the direction of the spinning.

In most cases where I have used the Geometric Technique, the client has had a very severe case of PTSD or some kind of traumatic event in the past.

I usually start with the Meta model, then as we start to uncover challenges, I intervene and use an appropriate NLP technique to alleviate the feeling. Once we reach the core challenge that is creating the anxiety, fear, or negative feeling, I work with the client using the appropriate NLP techniques to address the particular issue, before using the Geometric Technique to completely eliminate the anxiety.

I then go through validating with the client to ensure that the feeling has completely changed. I then guide the client through future pacing to ensure the complete success of the technique.

No Movement

After using the technique for several months, I experimented further with the sub modalities of the feelings. This was very important especially since many clients did not see the feeling as moving at all.

In many situations, the client would describe the stress feeling as a block of cement on their chest, or a block of solid material without moving but rather is very dense and heavy. It could be on the chest, or on the head.

Many times the feelings are described as a hand gripping the heart, or something holding the head or even the neck. Sometimes the feelings are described as squeezing or having a very solid grip.

In all these instances, there was no movement whatsoever.

Changing the color, the shape and creating movement worked well, but somehow I felt there was more that I could do to remove those feelings forever.

Transforming the Material

The one thing that I adapted further was the material from which the feelings were made. I would

Jihad Abou Zeid　　　　　　　　　　　　　　　www.FikrTraining.com

ask the client to describe the material of the feeling, and most of the time it was some heavy material like cement, or sometimes like wires or even metal pipes.

In some cases the feeling was described to be made from glass and has a pricking feeling to it.

I would then ask the client to change the shape of the feeling, and as the shape is changing, I ask them to change the material of the feeling as well. In most cases, I would ask them to change the material to playing dough, where it becomes very easy to just roll it out of the body.

The process starts by asking the client to tell me about their feelings, if it has a path, or not, where it starts and where it moves (if it does indeed move). I would then ask them to describe the material and color.

Jihad Abou Zeid www.FikrTraining.com

I would then start by asking them about their favorite color, and ask them to change the feeling to their favorite color. Then I ask them to change the shape and the movement (if it has a movement). If it is not moving, I ask them to create a movement, and to change the material to either playing dough, or sometimes to liquid, or even to a colored gas, or

Jihad Abou Zeid   www.FikrTraining.com

to any other material that is light and easy to remove. I decide on the material to use depending on the location and material that exists in the client's description. If for example the client describes the feeling as clinging and sticking on them, I would not use dough, instead I would change it to liquid, so it can easily slide off.

Using such changes usually helps relieve the feeling of stress and anxiety. However the technique does not stop there, I further ask the client to roll the dough out of their body. Or to use both hands and remove the dough from their body and to roll it into a small ball between their hands.

I ask them to continue removing the play dough until none is left, then I ask them to squeeze the ball between their hands so much until it changes into a silver coin, at which time I ask them to flip the coin very fast on the ground and then shoot it like a ball into space and up to the sun to melt and disappear (a technique used by Richard Bandler).

Usually this works like wonders. I then test the feelings of the client. I ask them to tell me how they feel at that moment. Almost always the client feels much lighter and says that the feeling has disappeared.

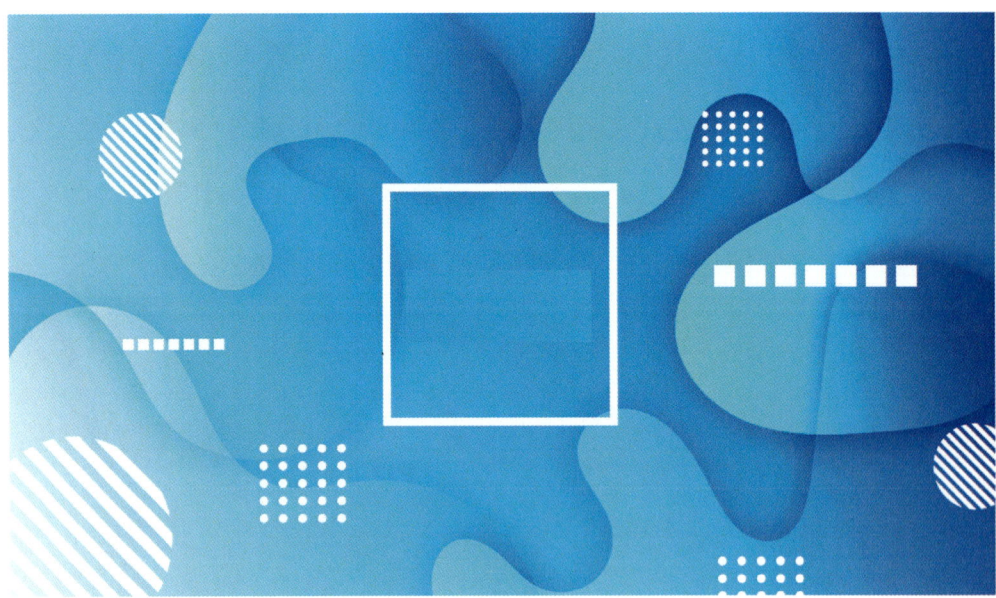

Jihad Abou Zeid   www.FikrTraining.com

Chasing the feelings

I then test the results by asking the client to search some more for the feeling, as sometimes severe stress or anxiety can hide in other places. I guide the client to search everywhere for any hidden feelings and I ask them to chase those feelings. If any are found, the technique is repeated, until there is no more stress or anxiety left.

The Vacuum Technique

Other techniques I have used to remove the feeling after changing the material to liquid, or to dust, is by asking the client to imagine a huge vacuum cleaner, and to hold the hose to suck out the liquid and then throw it out at the other end directly to the sun where I ask the client to see the liquid evaporating by the sun and disappearing leaving behind sparkles and colored bubbles popping into the sun.

Sound Effects

Sometimes I add some sound effects to make the vacuum cleaner sound, or the popping sound of the bubbles, this usually helps the clients to visualize better.

Stiff Grip

Clients that describe the feeling as a having a stiff grip on the chest, heart, head, neck or other places, I would first change the color, then the material of the feeling so that it eases the grip. I would then ask the client to use his hands and to break the grip by softly opening up the grip and at the same time removing the play dough.

Sometimes just by changing the material to a liquid with the client's favorite color, I then tell them to see the liquid just falling off their head, chest, or wherever it has been holding them. This works towards immediate relief and the client immediately feels free and light.

So far, I have a 100% success rate in all the cases that I have used the Geometric technique, and even in the most difficult cases, one or maximum two sessions were enough to completely change the feelings and remove the anxiety / stress and related feelings.

Feel free to experiment with the Geometric Technique, and I would love to hear from other NLP therapist if they also get the same results. It would also be very interesting if other NLP practitioners would perhaps experiment and develop further methods to enhance this powerful technique.

For consultations and one to one NLP sessions in helping get rid of stress, anxiety, PTSD, anger management, relationship issues, heart break, depression, fears, and other challenges, you can contact Jihad Abou Zeid directly on

fikr@fikrtraining.com to book a Skype session.

Made in the USA
Coppell, TX
30 March 2021